Into the
WINDS
of
HEAVEN

Christopher Beaudry

ISBN 978-1-68570-206-9 (paperback)
ISBN 978-1-68570-843-6 (hardcover)
ISBN 978-1-68570-207-6 (digital)

Christian Faith Publishing
832 Park Avenue
Meadville, PA 16335
www.christianfaithpublishing.com

Printed in the United States of America

ACKNOWLEDGEMENTS

To Lance, Derek, and Tarah
You have stood strong with me through the many winds we have
   walked together.
My prayer is that you always feel the presence of God as we walk
   through many more.

Thank you, Mom, for your lifetime encouragement.
Thank you, Caleigh, for your guidance and soul-touching support.
Thank you, Lynn, for your love and gentle peace.

EAST WINDS

He got up, rebuked the wind and said to the waves, "Quiet! Be still!" Then the wind died down and it was completely calm.
—Mark 4:39 (NIV)

The wind is howling
like this swirling storm inside
Couldn't keep it in
Heaven knows I tried

(*Frozen*, "Let It Go")

Your wonder of what is to become, your prayers that need to be answered. I hope your life goes the way of your dream; I hope the freedom that you've been given becomes the peace that you've searched for.

For what it's worth, it's never too late to become whoever you want to be. I hope your heart leads you to the promise...to your full soul potential...to your God-gifted purpose.

For it is love that will forever identify you, and it is love that will show the significance you will play in the world around you and in the world to come.

I wish you strength and gentleness, to laugh as much as you can and to cry as often as you need to.
Be kind to everyone because it matters; it always matters... You have been given a light to shine love and grace throughout your life. Light it up every chance you can because the shadows of evil will never stop chasing you.

I hope that you can forgive yourself for the dark past that sometimes creeps back into your mind.
Let it go and take one step at a time, one faith forward.
Remember, I'll always be there for you as I know you'll always be there for me.

I hope for a divine breeze in every breath you take. I hope for your future, joy, and prosperity.
I hope your destiny embraces the call to eternity and I hope all the wonders of who you become
will be answered by your prayers and mine.

And finally, I pray and hope that you find true love. Go be free, live your life, dream,
and always believe in forever. To God, all the glory...any way the wind blows.

Upon this rock, I stand and pray for the United States of America.
Upon this rock, I reflect on who I have become
with the freedoms I have been given and the position I hold as your
symbol of hope and peace.

I have soared to heights that many in this world will never reach.
I have flown in the darkness of war, and I have flown in the morning
sunlight of prosperity.
Through both, I have seen victories glow of liberty and the glory of
God almighty.

But I have also seen that the truth can be mistaken
by cloudy interpretation and politically confusing correctness.
I have seen character slowly diminish from souls
and fade into the unknown little hearts and minds of our children,
and I wonder, sometimes, if my wings are strong enough to protect
them.

I have stood tall upon the flagpole of the red, white, and blue,
and I have cried eagle tears with you when terror and death
have taken away our mothers and fathers, sisters and brothers.

So upon this rock, I will stand and pray for the United States of America, and it is by faith, and faith alone, that when I take flight again on this fourth day of July, your hope can be restored and celebrated, and you can believe in the truth...and in freedom again... freedom that always has been and always will be a gift of love from God, our Father, the same God of our founding fathers.

Please, pray with me...within your own faith, beneath your own tears, and upon your own rock.
God bless America!

If there are to be a thousand steps
between my fears and peace,
let me walk beside you,
let me search your mind.

I have some questions about hope
and thoughts I can't explain,
let me learn about your love
that I may love like you.

Show me with each step we take
how my journey truly matters,
show me how to leave behind
the fears that cause me pain,
and let me find the peace I seek
a thousand steps ahead.

You see, son, music is the pathway of our dreams and purpose,
and as we walk toward this beautiful light, we will begin to hear the
sacred sounds of our hearts.
If you listen to it quietly, you will understand how the six strings on
your guitar symbolize
the six wonders of your soul: courage, kindness, humility, peace,
faith, and love.
It's when you combine them into a sweet melody and into a strong
godly character that you'll realize how to play the songs of truth and
life and one day be able to play them in heaven.

Keep practicing, my son, it takes time to learn the songs of purpose,
and I'll always be there to play alongside you and help you follow
your dreams.
If you continue to have God as your teacher in life, the sounds will
forever play
in your heart and in the hearts of many others who listen to your
beautiful music.
I love you, son.

But, Mom, I just want to play a cool country song about walking down a path
with the sun in our faces... And hopefully, one day, I'll be as good as you are.
I love you too, Mom.

Sometimes, we need to allow the gift of silence into our lives.
To listen for the voice of God to speak
That He may share the secrets He has set aside for you.
To whisper softly into your soul that your heart is sacred to Him.
To offer a peace that has been missing amongst the natural noises of life,
Peace that will cradle you within the natural noises.
In the silence, you can feel His grace surround you and protect you
from fears and worries.
In the silence, your confidence can begin to grow into the humble,
wonderful, beautiful you.

Take some time in your days ahead to seek a little silence and find a
little peace.

While we graciously wait on the road to destiny,
>With love bursting out of our healing hearts,
>Let us pray for a new strength and a *wow* of our being and purpose.
>Let us play our song over and over again.

We need to dance to the beauty of us,
>And discover, once again, the childlike spirit embracing our souls.
>And let us dance on this journey with dream rhythm, step by hopeful step,
>With a grateful beat and a reflective flow of confidence and peace,
>And an endless chorus of love, sweet love.

The road ahead will still be long and winding,
>But with hearts like ours and a God-given second chance,
>The road we travel together will always be the road
>Where the music never ends,
>And the dancing never stops.

I'll continue to pray for you,
I hope you don't mind.
A gentle whisper
can bring you hope.
I just want to be your hero
and give God the glory.
Just let me show you
that broken hearts can mend.

Maybe we could take a walk
to find ourselves
and then be friends.
It's only temporary,
the pain you feel.
There's nothing ahead
that you should fear.

If I don't get to help you,
my purpose dims to dark.
I just want to walk in peace

and light the footprints
from the past.
So we can see each other
and walk in grace
and laugh a little.

Maybe together
the world makes sense.
There's still a story to tell,
deep within your soul.
I can see it in your eyes,
you lost your freedom,
just like me,
but now the truth
must face the lies.

I'll be you, and you'll be me,
and we can live again.
Let me be your hero.
Let me show you love.
I'll keep praying for you,
and if you don't mind,
will you pray for me?

Out in the rain, my soul learns to cry, no quiver, no worry, no wonder of why.

I sit and I pray softly into the wind for grace to embrace me and love to begin.

Out in the rain, I know I'll find peace from fear and from failure that must be released.

My umbrella covers me with blessings of hope and faith, now controls the life that I cope.

Thunder…hear me… I'm much louder than you! Lightning…see me… I'm much brighter than you!

I'm not afraid to be out in the rain! My spirit will cleanse me brand new!

Out in the rain, the truth I receive. Every drop is a reason I need to believe.

Time cannot flood any part of my dream. Dark grey clouds are never what they seem.

Out in the rain, I'm never alone. For God is in my heart, and He is my home.

I sit on the porch and wait for the day for the sun to come out and shine over my way.

Thunder…listen to me… I'm much stronger than you! Lightning… look at me… I'm much brighter than you!

I'm not afraid to be out in the rain! These skies will soon turn blue!

Out in the rain, my tears find my soul. In order to love, I must continue to grow.

Out in the rain, it's peace that finds me with a plan and a purpose to live and be free!

It's not about me; it's about who directs my heart.
The more I seek and pray to grow in character, the lesser man I become.
I don't mean to impose my words on others; I just want to propose peace and love and laughter because I believe it is God's plan for me from His own words.

I don't mean to always play the optimist and sing of joy
and dance along the streets of a good life,
and I don't want to share pessimism and struggle in the dirt with despair and darkness either.
I just want a little balance of both, a balance of truth.
I know that we live in a broken and fallen world, and I have a strong faith in an all-powerful God,
a God that can fix and heal everything. I want to see the eternal light shine within my eternal soul, even though darkness surrounds me every day, and I want that for you.

It's not all about me, although it used to be, and I'm really sorry for that.
I need to confront evil face-to-face now, but I'm still learning to fully understand its grasp on me.

I need to embrace love and carry it as my shield and strength and use it for God's purpose,
to help any lost and lonely souls.

I'm not going to exist anymore just to hope for happiness and success.
I now realize I'm here to share God's wisdom and truth
that He has graciously shared with me, and for that, I am grateful and honored.
It's not about me, it never was, and it never will be.
It's always been about the creator of my heart and the creator of yours.

A year has passed since I made the decision to walk down a new path, and as I surrendered to God,
I immediately felt peace pierce through the unopened door of my soul.
Confident and faithful that God's unpredictable plans would take me into a windstorm of love
with patience and purpose and, perhaps, a few old heartbroken tears.

I followed along and prayed, and while I was walking and praying…
an old friend from forty years past gently wandered onto my quiet path.
Perhaps she was on her own silent search to surrender to God,
to seek and find serenity from a life of broken dreams and misunderstandings?

Perhaps she just needed to walk and let the wind blow open the door of her soul
Where she could feel, once again, the spirit of love?
We both needed a friend that day. We both needed a walk to free ourselves
from lost yesterdays and the worries of many tomorrows.
We talked of memories and children and puppies and songs.

We laughed as though we were forty years younger and our dreams were still up ahead.
And life was beautiful because we allowed God to walk alongside us, surrounding us with His graceful wind, teaching us of His truth, and reminding us how wonderful love truly is.

It's been an amazing, blessed year.
And as we continue to walk down our path of peace, into the wind, our future is guided by hope, where the doors of our souls are wide open
so that God's love will always be welcomed.
Thank you for choosing this path with me, and thank you, God, for answering our prayers
and creating this beautiful new journey so we can walk in peace, embracing love until eternity calls.

Sometimes I put on my sweatshirt inside out
when I'm home alone
'cause I think it looks cool.

Sometimes I wear two pairs of socks
with my Friday-night boots
cause it builds my confidence and I dance better.

Sometimes I wish I could go back in time
to high school and do a few things differently,
but the memories are still incredibly good enough.

Sometimes I let my heart break
to make it better the next time.
Sometimes I find my soul
when I'm not even looking for it.

Sometimes I do stupid things
and cling to forgiveness, and then
just watch silly geese wandering around at sunset.
Sometimes life is good,
and sometimes it's not,
        but I always thank God
        for every one of my sometimes
        any way the wind blows.

I come to the cross today, Lord, to pray…to feel your presence within my soul.
I come to the cross today, Lord, to thank you for every breath I've ever taken.

Embrace me with your Holy blood. Grace me with your constant love.
Show me how to live again. Know me when I need a friend.
Cleanse my heart and wipe my tears. Release more faith and erase my fears.
Forgive me for the dark I've done, and light my way toward your Son.

I come to the cross today, Lord, to pray for healing and hope and heavenly peace.
I come to the cross today, Lord, to thank you for every word you've ever given.

Bless my family, bless my friends.
for whatever cross that they may carry
show them the love you've shown to me, show them the truth, and
set them free.

In Jesus's name. Amen.

Love has many rocks to conquer, and until we can reach the top...
we may never know the profound truth of our heart.
That rare radical love that we breathe into our soul to find peace,
that kind of love that transforms us to see people the way God sees
them,
a love that requires you to take others to the top.
No matter how difficult the climb and no matter how afraid you are
to continue,
I pray for all of us to keep climbing, keep loving, and keep rocking!

You might be believing that nothing makes sense
with one day of burden, you're climbing the fence
it's not what you thought it would be over here
it's much more dramatic and layered in fear.

You can't understand why the world is all mad
when we all disagree with what's good and what's bad
if seeing is truth, and the truth sets us free
then why is there freedom we can't even see?

You find yourself hoping that it's better tomorrow
for your shame and guilt to get washed in your sorrow
and what if your dreams are much farther to reach
and what will we learn if there's no one to teach.

You roll with the changes and rock till you drop
until something inside you screams softly to stop
your heart begins beating like drums to your soul
and you can't tell the difference if you're young or you're old.

You might have a chance to finish this race
if determined to fight and lean on God's grace
with patience and love and a purpose to live
your weak is His strength; your take is His give.

You might be believing that everything makes sense
with one day of joy; you're climbing the fence
and faith you've discovered is on either side
where peace is released and fear has now died.

You know that it's Friday, and I'm feeling the rhyme
to call on my friends to love all the time
so have a blessed weekend, some highs and some lows
and remember to laugh…any way the wind blows.

My April wind, come close to me.
I want to feel your breath upon my face.
I want to look deeply above and far beyond your skies and see what you see.

My April rain, do not be afraid to cry with me.
I want to know your true love and saddened spirit.
I want to cleanse your heart and bring bright colors to your soul.

April, my sweet April, hold on to hope and beautification in the shining sun.
April, my dear April, walk with me gently until May, but never let me go.

Those forbidden places and the neglect of peace, shadows and storms, and the rain does not cease.
Dust and dark kingdoms, no sight that there's hope, lost and exposed where the heart cannot cope.

It's suffering you seek; you think you're too weak that your troubles are everyone else.
It's all just a lie and you're questioning why, 'cause you're living so full of yourself.

Stop all this nonsense, and don't be afraid. The places I'll take you are heavenly made.
I'll show you love and a passion to care. I'll teach you to dream till your soul is aware.

I'll walk with you daily as your joy is increased, to the end of your journey, where your heart will find peace.
So please come along, I'll help you get strong, and your shadow will fade in the sun.

Life's going to be fine 'cause I made you shine for the glory of the almighty one.

The decisions we make every day help determine the direction of our true selves.
Will they take us down the path of our destiny?
Will they deliver us to our hope-filled divine dreams? Can we dance along the way?

Decisions, decisions.
Right ones, wrong ones.
Short ones, long ones.
Green ones, blue ones.
Me ones, you ones.

Oh, the decisions we make of danger and desire
May lead us to darkness and into the fire.
Oh, the decisions we make of respect and love
Will take us to places like heaven above.
And the truth we shall find with choices and chance
Down the pathway of dreams, where yes, we can dance.

Decisions, decisions.
Good ones, bad ones.
Fun ones, sad ones.
Mean ones, kind ones.
Heart ones, mind ones.

SOUTH WINDS

But when he saw the wind, he was afraid and, beginning
to sink, cried out, "Lord, save me!"
—Matthew 14:30 (NIV)

I listen to the wind
to the wind of my soul
Where I'll end up, well,
I think only God really knows.

(Cat Stevens, "The Wind")

Truth is above time and space, but nothing is impossible with God. We all have a will, gifted to us freely. We have a love from above that resides within us.
It embraces our hearts and minds and dwells within our souls.
Love gives us the strength by the spirit of light to choose and shine it toward others, our choice.

Although absolute truth is above our comprehension, we are made to seek it. This perpetual pursuit and process are for our distinct purpose in life; it's for all of us to discover faith in our way of hope and recognize the amazing power blessed upon us by one voice.

Sometimes we need to rediscover ourselves when our progress slows down and gets tainted by a worldview that defines truth based on a personal agenda: a selfish, spiritless vision. We must bring back the ancient eternal wisdom of a world full of beauty and peace, a world that practices
"In God We Trust," a world where we sit beside Him, learn of love and forgiveness, and learn to rejoice.

There's a new generation that needs to hear the truth, an existing generation that includes all of us, that needs to listen to our hearts and take on the responsibility to teach the truth and continue to seek it out through love. Truth is out there with plenty of time to be reached and enough space to stretch out our hands and embrace it; it is God's will, but it is our choice.

Any way the wind blows…

A tear or two is all I need right now, a tear and my heart can finally see.
If I replay all the memories of you, there's peace within my mind.

As I wipe away my worries, a vision of hope, I find.
If it teaches me to love again and become who I used to be,
I'll wipe away my wonders and set my soul flying free.
I'm just a tear away from love. I'm just a tear away from you.

Two tears are all I need right now: one for you and one for me
Take my heart and look inside to feel what I can see.

I recently began trying to untangle my memories of the seventies and all the reasons I did what I did. I've been trying to unearth my footprints as I trace those dream-filled years
up the mountain I still currently climb.

Slowly, I begin to weave through the fibers of old fears as I watch the fallen pieces of my lost identity begin to take hold of my heart. The world I knew then is not the world I know now, and that's okay.

As I look back, I've discovered a thousand gifts that have been stored within the grace-filled
fabric of my soul. As I open them up, a whole new perspective lined with passion and peace
begins to clear up my life's meaning, recognizing now that the person I was then
is still the person I am now, only much closer to God.

Knowing that the purpose and significance of the seventies was a
process planned to teach me to love, to belong, to become, and to
believe in the truth of my being, to share the knowledge
of wonder and wisdom with the world around me.

I am forever grateful to my family and friends for allowing me to
walk alongside them,
making footprints and memories, and I thank God for the strength
and the courage and the grace
so that I could and still can keep climbing the mountain of my
dreams.

Sometimes the harsh touch of impossibilities is what God uses to hold us tight to His heart while He silently teaches us to trust, no matter what lies outside our window of life.

When hearts are broken and loneliness leads your tears to places of doubt, and you seek the why by dwelling on empty promises and lost or forgotten dreams, remember, God is holding you.

Sometimes hope can be difficult to download when what is directly in front of you is dark and ugly, and pain surrounds your suffering with sadness, and you wonder how your soul could ever survive, and all you want to do is give up and let go.

Hold on, my friend, because God is holding you, and He will never let you go.
With the breath of His grace, He will lift you up high and into the spiritual healing wind of heaven.
Hold on, He has a plan, and it begins in your heart for the purpose of love, forever.

Sometimes, the soft touch of possibilities is what God uses to hold us tight to His heart while He quietly teaches us to love, no matter what happens outside our window of life.

Faith doesn't always make sense.
Our beliefs and doubts often swirl around intimately in both hesitant breezes and courageous winds together yet always changing.
The world is both brutal and beautiful; we're tickled and taunted at the same time.
Hints of grace, glimmer in the darkness, hope whispers through our pain.
Hearts are broken, souls are bruised, but still, love sometimes wins.
We laugh and we cry, then we dream to live another day, wondering about the purpose of tomorrow.

Life doesn't always make sense.
That's why we need faith.
It lets us know that we are always loved, into the winds of heaven.

May we defend with diligence the brightest light of our dreams.
May we defeat our disappointments and direct them into the darkness.
May we be delivered to our destiny as it was always designed.
And may we dance all the days of our lives.

The winds of heaven have blown my way over the past couple of years and cooled down my perspective on things. Allow me to share a few words on a subject in which God has shown me to be a critical and important character, calling on mine and hopefully yours on the education of soul and spirit.

Bear with me.

Learning to use the gift of gentleness is essential as we face adversities and try to power through our everyday relationships and our everyday circumstances. Some may think of it as a weakness, but being gentle is a sign of glory and strength, a sort of graceful journey on an unknown, unpredictable path with a bold and determined goal.

Gentleness begins with a slow elimination of complaining, criticizing, and comparing, then transitions to seeking a beautiful surrender to purpose and peace. It's growing and becoming who you truly are through the process of identifying the deepest desires of your own heart. It's moving forward by humbling yourself and listening to the broken hearts of others.

Learning to be gentle is a prerequisite to love, and I hope and pray, my dear friends, that throughout this new school year, you learn to feel the gentle winds of heaven blow through your heart while you continue your studies on spirit and soul.

Have faith and bear in mind, you have the greatest teacher in the world with a supernatural almighty degree in love. God bless!

I write of peace as though I've walked ahead of my shadow in the brightness of a promised path toward some unforeseen spiritual destiny. But many times, I became lost in words, afraid to continue on, doubting the purpose of my journey. I've wondered why I still hear echoes of weakness, in and out of the darkness, in and out of my life, and in and out of the world around me.

If I could somehow see this timeless truth by stopping long enough to rest, to allow myself to be a child again, to dream and unleash the playful poet who sits quietly at the unlocked door of my heart, waiting with passion and energy to dance out the door laughing, to dance down the destined path to peace in pursuit of all the possibilities God has to offer me and to help others unlock the doors of their own misunderstood hearts.

Sometimes I just stare down the future life path in front of me and think, "All I can do is *pray* and let God (with His powerful *love*) piece together, moment by moment, the *peace* I long for...the peace that flows in the silence of Heaven...to *trust* Him for teaching me *patience*, granting me *grace*, and singing to my soul a song of *courage* and *hope*, and blessing my journey along the way…that I may share my gifts in the shadow of His shining *love* and keep walking in *faith* and never turning back."

Every day, each one of us creates new hours of history.
　　Hours that in time mean something in this world.
　　Hours that say, "Maybe one day, our hopes will become real and true,
　　and we'll realize that life does actually matter."
Every day, we have a choice to be a part of history,
　　a part of paradise and providence and peace,
　　a choice to love one another, no matter where we live in this world,
　　a choice that will impact our life and its eternal purpose.
　　Every day your life truly matters.

Every day, the world needs you.
And every day is, always, a good day.

The realm of my imagination covers all the wonders of my heaven within the ripples of my journey, flows the spirit of my wild child amazed at every river's turn, I see a world of beautiful love.

I see dragons picking daisies
and turtles playing hoop.
I see truth being honored
while lies turn to poop.

I see gardens grow forever
and an unlocked gate.
There are falcons and cheesecake
and the extinction of hate.

I see mountains and oceans
switching places for funs.
I befriended a goldfish
who told stories with puns.

I see wizards slash worries
and angels sing hope.
I never get dirty, so
there's no need for soap.

There are sunsets and sunrises
seem like every half hour.
Everyone's like family,
and no one seeks power.

The ants protect shorelines
from devils and looters.
Nothing gets broken,
not hearts nor computers.

I see reasons to live;
I see reasons to die;
I see faith as the answer
when the question is *why?*

The realm of my imagination surrounds the grace within my bottle
beyond the ripples of my destiny flows the peace of a grateful child
amazed at every river's turn, I see heaven, and I see love.

Out in the mist lies our hope of a beautiful day,
Our spirit barks softly and awakens our souls,
Our tails wag recklessly with wonder and love,
We're ready to fetch whatever God throws.

I am content within my Fence.
It's where you touched my soul
I may not be as strong as you
but I still have time to grow.

I am content without much Fear,
We've each been blessed a story
our past may be forgiven now
our hope will rest with glory.

I am content behind this Face.
My smile lies deep in my heart,
look inside my peaceful eyes
to see we're not so far apart.

I am content by way of Faith
to trust what I cannot see
for nothing could ever divide our love
for it is God who sets us free.

Thank you for the breath of life that I may speak often from my heart.

Thank you for the pain of death and darkness that I may learn to grow by faith.

Thank you for the laughter and tears and all the moments in between and for believing in me since the day I was born.

Thank you for broken hearts and second chances and blessings that I first thought were troubles and worries and failures.

Thank you for the times I was lost, times that I was searching for the promise of you and then realizing that you were right beside me all along.

Thank you for the sleepless nights, the restless parties with the welcomed wake-up call from grace, and for the blood-stained cross I wear on my neck.

And finally, thank you for loving me and teaching me to love you, by loving others.

It is love that I must forever speak of, it is love that keeps me breathing, and it is love that I am most thankful for, into the winds of heaven.

As I grow older as a father, I believe I am becoming a better student in the observation of life. The purposes and significance of every moment presented to me. There rises a great truth within me that lights my way with enthusiasm and sincerity and pushes.me to continue to teach my children not only about the world they live in but also the eternal world to come.

To believe in who they are, to succeed in becoming the person they are supposed to become and to love every moment they walk and breathe.

So here is my little learning list of love lines to my sons, to my daughters, to my blessings, and to all others who dare to dream:

1. Always stand up for what you're *for*, not for what you're against.
2. It hurts to fail, but the pain is worse if you never *try again*.
3. Make sure your *character growth* is a higher priority than your financial growth.
4. When things are sad, *pray*. When things are happy, *be thankful*. When things are in between, *do both*.

5. Be *gentle* and *strong*, have *courage* and *empathy*. Others will need you, be friends with everyone.

6. *Appreciate* the moon and the stars, sunsets and sunrises, and all the sounds and sights of *nature* the wind may offer.

7. It is not so much that you need to know more; you just have to *do more with what you know.*

8. *Never lose* the heart and wonder of *childhood,* no matter the pressures and stresses of adulthood.

9. Find things you may not even be looking for and *experience the joy of discovery again* and again.

10. Read, observe, and study daily, including the Bible, and *never stop learning to learn.*

11. *Dance, laugh, and sing;* let the music you hear always flow through your heart and into your soul.

12. In your relationships and marriages, remember that the phrases "I'm sorry" and "I forgive you" are *just as important* as "I love you."

Finally, as much as I love you all, *God loves you more.*

And so the missing piece of all you are seems to be somewhere else
at some other time,
and all you can do is wonder why and decide whether or not you're
going to cry.
It's as if you can't really understand the logic in your heart and in
which direction
your dream is supposed to take you or whether or not you even have
the right dream.

Perhaps all you really need
is a little faith
and a little time
to realize that the piece you're missing
is the peace within you.

There are times we must escape into the north, into the woods, into the soft gray of the skies
and allow the rain to fall upon our face and begin the cleansing of our soul.

There are times we must encounter memories of our past, moments of our childhood,
memories of the adventures we sought searching for the sun, seeking to exist as God scheduled.

There are times that life must be enjoyed without the worry, without the tears, without the concerns of the unknown tomorrows…with only the laughter of walking with the wind, with love in your heart.

Escape… Encounter… Enjoy

Love only appears to us in two ways:
From above and from within;
And therein lies the connection,
For a beautiful relationship.
Into the winds of heaven.

WEST WINDS

When he thunders, the waters in the heavens roar; he
makes clouds rise from the ends of the earth.
He sends lightning with the rain and brings
out the wind from his storehouses.
                                        —Jeremiah 10:13 (NIV)

High on this mountain, the clouds down below
I'm feeling so strong and alive
From this rocky perch, I'll continue to search
for the wind and the snow and the sky

(Dan Fogelberg, "Netherlands")

I don't want tomorrow to see me,
the way that I am today.

Less is my hope, asleep is my soul
and I've lost my wonder and way.

But give me a moment,
to spark up my spirit,
and awaken my heart to play.

Show me your eyes of glory
and gently touch me with your grace.
Remind me that I just need to love you
and listen to you while I pray.

Sometimes, we need to seek a quiet place to rest our troubled hearts,
a place along the sands of time and truth,
a place that will tolerate our constant questioning of the wounds of
love.

Sometimes, we need a place that offers wisdom and a light
to the dark misunderstanding of forgiveness,
a place of tender mercy and unconditional acceptance,
a place of comfort and peace.

And sometimes we need a place to pray and generate joy and process
hope,
a place where we can find faith, a place where we can grow angel wings

and believe that one day, our hearts will soar higher than we could
ever have known,
a place where no one can see us cry…
except God.

You may feel as though you're drowning in the deep end of your life
and the rains keep falling, with no sign of relief.
Remember, with God, all things are possible.
His grace is like gentle wings of beauty,
and His love is strong enough to lift you above any of your circumstances.
Have faith that He will carry you out of these deep waters
with a secure flight from adversity into blessings
from darkness into a light of hope and peace.

Never give up, my friends.
Stretch out your hand in faith.
Breathe again and fly.

Every human heart will cry in the process of seeking truth…
the rich, the powerful, the poor, the helpless, both you and I.
We must never allow these tears to wash away our hope in humanity
or our faith in forever.

God is the truth, and if we abandon this principle, we will soon get
stuck and tangled in a faithless way of life, simply coping in a fallen
world and never discovering our true identity or purpose,
never resolving any of our daily differences.

Truth is love, and when we live it and share it with other people and
the world around us,
life becomes meaningful, peace is reachable, and salvation
becomes burned into our soul by the fire of the Holy Spirit forever.

Every human heart will die in the process of seeking truth.
Let's be encouraged to keep seeking; let's be forgiven, and let's forgive
others.
Let's believe in the truth now. Let's live for the call to eternity.

Sometimes, when we've been hurt, we go off to sit in a corner for a little while for a playful time-out where the lights seem to twinkle with peace and our thoughts go into wonder.

Sometimes, we feel like crying, but we can't, and sometimes we try not to cry, but we do, and either way, the tears begin to fall within our soul and sacred silence, and our hopes go far off into wonder.

Sometimes, our doubts will search our desperate hearts to try and understand all the mysteries of love, and whether or not love will ever understand us, and then both fear and faith turn into wonder.

Sometimes, we wish we could become children again, where we could just enjoy the twinkling of the lights in the process of regrowing our hearts again with peace and imagination, to love and wonder.

Our passionate heart is the core principle of our survival and growth
and the essence of every heart always embodies love.
We cannot forget that love is a choice.

A choice we need to make
every morning when we get up
and every night before we sleep
and every waking moment in between.
Love is...when you give and give,
even when you don't think
you can give anymore.
Love is...keeping the faith when the pain seems unbearable.

Love listens to the laughter. Love listens to the tears. Love listens to
every word
and every sound of silence while you search your soul.
Love is God's greatest blessing to our existence,
and the essence of love can only grow from the seedlings in our hearts.

You are the light of my world,
You are the blue in my skies,
You are my mountain and
I am one grain of sand.

You are the breeze in my storm,
You are the gentle in my pain,
You are my ocean and
I am one single tear.

Here is my heart, Lord, broken and cold,
Exposed by my fears and still growing old.

Here is my prayer, Lord, simple and raw,
Teach me to love you, full of wonder and awe.

You are the strength for my spirit,
You are the grace for my peace,
You are my forever, and
I am one moment in time.

Remember, my child, you have a beautiful soul that will forever matter in this life.
You have been touched by the light of pure grace; you have been given the honor to carry this light and shine love wherever you go, wherever the wind may take you.

There are things of this world that will eventually reveal dark days and sadness, and one day your heart will be broken, you may get lost in the wild of senseless struggles, and rejection will find you standing in the shadows of lonely. Tears will fall.

My sweet child, as your Spirit, I will never leave you; I will always walk beside you.
I will teach you to be brave and courageous; I will bless you with peace.
Together, we will grow stronger and wiser; we will overcome with amazing joy.
We will build our hope and heal into the truth of who you really are, a beautiful soul, a beautiful daughter of God, and the shining light of my love.

Sometimes we barely hold onto the frail, ragged ends of our hopes
and sometimes we just search out a place to hide
and the wonder within us seems to fade into doubt
and we believe that our desires and dreams may have died.

When our spirit grows faint, and we can't seem to shake it
and the darkness of life heightens shadows and fears
the troubles, we worry, will get tangled in lies
and we can no longer see our true selves in the mirror.

Take a deep breath and allow peace into your heart
let the disappointments become discoveries of grace.
Persevere with faith as you gain strength and grow
and wipe away the vulnerable tears from your face.

There's a power we have that we might not have known.
Let's shift ourselves forward and declare ourselves ready
for our actual purpose where love guides our way
where our hopes are not wasted, and our souls are now steady.

Sometimes, we just need to hang on and make our way through and
know that we are never alone and thank God for that.

There's a certain emptiness that lies trapped within the heart of every person who's trying to understand loneliness despite being around many, many friends and who's questioning while wondering what real love is, if it's reachable or not, still hoping to be awakened from the darkness by a soul-sharing, shining light.

There's a certain fulfillment that always lingers within the heart of every person, feeling the presence of a spirit, freedom laced with peace, sprinkled with joy, and waiting for a thunderous explosion of laughter and light, and grasping at the innocent feeling of real love.

I suppose there's a certain truth that most of us have a heart that is somewhere between
empty and full, and whether we realize it or not, as long as there is something in there,
the potential to love will always exist; I am certain of that.

May the winds of your future blow blessings of peace and grace to you and your family.

May you embrace change: good or bad, and accept it as a challenge to grow and increase your integrity. May you view the world from the eyes of your heart and never allow bitter tears to fall.

May you confront your past with truth and purpose, seize it and let it soar into the wind of forgiveness, into the new clouds of hope, and into the hands of God.

May you never underestimate your potential to be. Life is a continuous process of learning.

May you always reach higher to obtain the heavenly gifts given and planned for you.

May you be anointed by the spirit within your soul to develop a calm and caring character built on patience and kindness, built on trust and faith, and built on a solid foundation of love.

May peace and grace follow you into your destiny.
May you and your family be blessed.
Into the winds of heaven.

So many songs I've played in my head while moving toward my destination.
My heart is filled with memories that overflow with peace beyond my understanding.

So many blessings have been bestowed to me along the path I've walked
that I feel overwhelmed by a love that makes me stronger every step I take.

So many dreams,
So many hopes,
So many reasons to keep walking,
So many more songs to play.

Our first lesson in our first moment of life was how to breathe.
And our first response to this new knowledge in this new world was
to cry.

It only took moments for us to learn our second lesson in life, how
to love.

No matter how old we are, no matter what we've been through, no
matter our failures,
No matter our pain, and no matter how many lessons this world has
taught us.
We must stop and take a moment to learn to breathe again.
Let out a big cry and allow the tears to fall into the peaceful bliss of
God.

And then love again.

If we don't know our potential to become,
our desire and drive to get anywhere weakens.
If we don't have the passion to love others,
our divine light will dim slowly into darkness.

If we don't seek the promise of peace and truth,
then we are allowing the world to do it for us,
which sends us into a state of confusion,
and a little misery of misunderstanding,
and it ultimately devours our hopes and happiness.

We must be the change.
We cannot be afraid to fight, our light must shine bright.
We cannot give up or give in,
but give we must from deep within
through the spirit, through the soul,
and through the awakening of our hearts.

We must give and keep giving.
We must encourage and challenge each other

to stretch out and grasp our potential with pure passion, to live out
our God-given promises.

If we don't know where our new path in life begins,
then we just keep walking, keep believing,
and keep looking for the sign that says,
"*Love.*"

I made a difference, and that difference made a difference in me.
My heart is where it needs to be now, my soul sings.
I found a love that somehow had been looking for me.
And that love helped me see how different I could be if I would just be me.
The me that God meant for me to be.

My friends, be yourself.
And don't be afraid to be different.
But always remember to do it with love.

Peace and Grace

Spilled across the canvas of our hopes are the colors of all our imperfections,
Dripping and splattering out of control outside the lines of normal,
Where we display the art of our God-gifted abilities
And expose the hurt of our self-proclaimed inabilities.

For peace of heart, we must learn to paint the portrait of our passions and purpose.
Allow the beauty of our soul to get up with calm, confident courage,
And dance into the masterpiece our creator intended, imperfections and all
For our work is still unfinished, our dreams are still being dreamt up,
And our bucket still holds all the colors of God's love and grace.

Keep painting colorfully, my friends.
It doesn't matter what you spill or splatter.
It only matters that you get up and dance,
And I hope and pray that you do.

My heart has a complete, vibrant rhythm about it, an inexperienced feeling of gentleness and strength. My life at this moment is true and significant, and if I can save it and nurture it into its potential, I know I will live forever.

You are my passionate counselor, guiding me to a light I have never seen before, shining brighter and brighter, bringing me to a divine awareness, an overwhelming sense of peace and joyful wonder.

I am confident within my soul that you are my angel of love, waiting to embrace me and take me from the sullen valleys of earth up to the glorious free-flowing rivers of heaven.

I am blessed beyond time,
I am yours…forever.

I am with you, my child. It's okay to be sad in this moment, but your heart is resting in my blessing now.

In order to grow, there will be tears that need to fall. There will be pain from your fractured soul that will happen unexpectedly. Your thoughts will wander into blame or guilt; some will flow into regret or sorrow. You will question your worth in this world, asking why your past needed to mess with your future. You will begin to fight forgiveness, and it will fight back, pulling you down into the dark and damned pit where you lie silent and sad.

My child, you are not broken. A light will shine soon. The shadow of my cross will appear before you; it will glow from within you, slowly healing you and protecting you eternally. You are my sweet and beautiful child. My perfect love has never been apart from you. Take a deep breath of hope and let out your faith; my spirit will lift you up and guide you through today and even higher tomorrow. Awaken to the purpose I have chosen for you. My grace will follow you wherever you go.

I give you my word, take it.
I give you my promise, trust me.
I give you my peace, live it.
I give you my light to take away all your sadness
so you can rest in my heart...forever.

NORTH WINDS

The wind blows wherever it pleases. You hear its sound,
but you cannot tell where it comes from or where it is
going. So it is with everyone born of the Spirit.

—John 3:8 (NIV)

Nothing really matters, anyone can see
Nothing really matters...
Nothing really matters to me...
Any way the wind blows...

(Queen, "Bohemian Rhapsody")

Let us accept the premise that we are governed by something far beyond this world
by something deeply rooted in the silent conscience of our soul.

Let us allow our hope to be sustained and guided through our every-day choices,
everyday dreams, and by the everyday people we meet.

Let us awaken our faith from the fallen sleep of fear and rub our tearful eyes
from the distorted spectacle of this world and redirect our vision to our chosen path.

Let us activate the goodness in our heart and let the gentle power of truth lift us high
and set us free into the peaceful presence of pure love.

And let us acknowledge and share that there truly is something out there,
far beyond this world and deep within our soul.

Don't give up.
Don't be discouraged by the distractions and difficulties of this world.
Don't be deceived by the dangers and developments of false fears and disappointments.
There is still a friend you haven't met yet, a friend who understands and listens
To the rhythm of your heart and the silence of your soul.

There is still a friend that God hasn't introduced to you yet.
He's waiting for that moment in time when His truth crisscrosses with your faith,
And the light of the spirit shines you blind, and a gentle peace surrounds your being,
And you can begin to walk down the center of your dream with confidence and joy.
Don't be discouraged.
Don't be deceived,
And don't ever give up.

I now know that there are treasures to find in the memories of our lives that can lead you from forgiveness to humility and offer you an honest helping of hope.

I now know that the lessons we have learned from the failures in our lives can always revive our once crushed and gentle spirit.

At my wise and wonderful age, I now know how to survive on a deserted island from my shipwrecked soul and still find the strength and courage to pick up the pieces of my heart that the storms of life have blown apart.

I now know that some dreams wither and some dreams flourish and some dreams
are still seedlings that are waiting to become.

I now know that love is patient and kind and 1/13th Corinthians, but it's also crazy and stupid, and sometimes, impossible to grasp, but when you do embrace it, it's beautiful to never let go, and I won't.

I now know that each year I celebrate my birth, it becomes easier to look forward to celebrating in heaven,
and as I continue to know everything about nothing and absolutely nothing about everything,
I'll continue to treasure my peace and joy and learn more about the purpose of my gentle spirit.

What I don't know is what tomorrow will bring, but my faith in God tells me I do. It's the truth and the trust in Him that truly explains the meaning of my life, and it's His grace that keeps me dreaming on.

May God bless you, my friends. Always treasure every moment of your life.

If we believe that our burdens will turn into blessings,
then we have found *faith*.

If we squander each day into wastefulness of worry,
then we have lost *hope*.

If we allow our spirit to speak directly to our soul,
then we have discovered *peace*,
and if we just listen to the song in our heart
and dance for the glory of the Lord,
then we will understand *love*.

There are times to reflect deep within the silence of our soul
to be truly honest with ourselves, to cleanse the mind of any insig-
nificant ways.

We must refocus our vision and reevaluate our values,
and believe that our potential is limitless as long as we continue to
learn and grow.

We cannot erase the sad moments that lie behind us
or worry about those moments that still loom on ahead; what's
important is what lies within us.

We still have a conscience, an inner guidance system of the heart,
where we can still imagine, where we can differentiate between right
and wrong, and where we love unconditionally.

There are times to stop along the road and pick up the little drops of
hope we may have lost before.

A time to relearn how to dream and then dream again,
A time to build character and set principles, and believe in our freedoms,
A time to just examine time for what it is. Life...perhaps the time is now... Live.

There are winds from the south and winds from the north, but the seasons never changed when the brothers were together.

Bunk bed raised, cornflakes fed, never an adventure without a story to tell; we were teammates in the sport of love and war, soldiers of hope and glory from our Sicilian souls and our farmer's hearts; we learned to travel both the chosen path and the forbidden fields, and each one lead us to the land of laughter and lessons learned from city to country, from rivers to lakes, and from late night binges of rock and roll, our blood always flowed together, and when one soldier went down, we banded together and prayed in a garden to fight and love even stronger.

There are winds from the east and winds from the west, but the seasons never changed when the brothers were together.
Any way the wind blows.

The first feel of shiver in a cool autumn rain
like the silent transformation of a heart grieving pain.

The darkness comes closer, and the light is much less,
there's a shift in our soul as we cry emptiness.

The leaves may be falling as well as the tears,
but trust in the wind to guide away fears.

It's a time to find freedom and the significance of peace,
a time to forgive and let God's love release.

If we count all our blessings one leaf at a time,
our shiver will warm, and the sun will then shine.

If we can learn to fly a kite without knowing the pattern of the wind, then perhaps, we can learn to trust without knowing the direction our lives will go.

We may still struggle to understand how our past has always been our guide for the next direction,

but it will always be important to trust in the creator of our wind and His purpose for our flight,

and in our freedom to soar as high as we can soar and as far as we can love.

Let us fly our kites in faith into the winds of heaven.

Your greatness has always been inside you, deep within the stillness of your soul, longing to shine the brightness of what's meant to be. You cannot allow fear to darken your dreams or let the past prevent you from God's purpose.

If you feel lost, lonely, or just left behind today, remember that you were born to be great, born to shine a bright light for others to see. Have faith in the greatness of you.

It's what you think about when you think about what's happened, what's next?
It's the heavenly voice letting you know that your life will flow, anyway, the wind will blow.
It's your destiny born from a dream blessed by
and nourished through the fullness of your faith.
It's your awakening of the heart.
It's your reason not only to live forever but to love forever.
It's what you think about.
It's why you hope for tomorrow.
It's why you believe in today,
and it's why it really doesn't matter what's next.

There's a place where the soul and spirit meet.

A place where the music whispers and trembles to the rhythm of your past,
Then leads you, in chorus, to the future and purpose of your life.

We can never be afraid to step out onto the dance floor.
We can never be afraid to dance.
A place where hearts are never broken,
A place where hope is never lost,
A place where love is what you breathe,
and if tears may fall
and memories flow in,
It's a place for comfort and peace from it all.

There's a place where the soul and spirit sing together.

So dance…and dance…and dance forever.

Love is a thousand memories.
I hope your good ones outshine the bad,
fill your hearts with lessons learned,
and God will bless everything you have.

Love is a thousand stories.
I hope that you can read them all,
read them with your fragile hearts,
and God will never let you fall.

Love is a thousand dreams.
I hope that you walk through them together,
share your souls with adventure and peace,
and God will guide you always and forever.

Believe in the goodness of your heart; you were born and destined to love.

There has always been a need for your contribution to this world.

It's your own top-shelf brand of beautiful,

your golden seal of significance,

your grace-covered gift from God,

always guiding you to love, to help others grow, to help them heal their brokenness, to give them hope, to smile and shine a light into their soul.

Believe in yourself, even if others don't, and even if you've been rejected, neglected, lost, or alone. Believe in the power of your heart. You were created to love,

no matter the circumstances in your life,

no matter the pain you've gone through,

no matter which way the wind blows.

Life isn't going to be fair; you must accept that, have faith that the heart knows the truth.

The story of love must forever continue, and you must work hard at it and believe in it.

Believe in the presence of God in your heart. Believe in yourself.

God believes in you, He always has, and that's why love always matters.

Hugs and peace, my friends.

It's been some time since I've been able to get an appointment to speak with my heart.
I've been away…far away, just hanging out with hope, drinking my sorrows away
with tall glasses of loneliness and a splash of lime
to feel the slight taste of bitterness that helps justify my pain and regret.

It's been a while since I sat down to talk to my heart.
I wonder if he is still capable of doing what he was destined to do?
If he is still gentle enough to show compassion to friends who are lost or lonely?
If he is quiet and grateful enough to listen to the wisdom of my world and pray to God when my wisdom goes wrong?

It's hard to remember the last time my heart was completely healed from the battle wounds of life
from all the cracks, scratches, and fractures compiled over many years
from trying to process the languages of love
while grasping at the belief that forgiveness is the key
to taking me to the sweet places of peace and truth.

But you know, I think I'm ready now to sit down and bond with my
heart.
I'm sure he's been waiting a long time to sit down with me too.
To remind me of my soul's purpose
and to show me how to love again
and I'm so looking forward to it.

I've been hanging out too much with my friends, Pride and Doubt. These two idiots seem to pressure and overwhelm me into building a "perfect" life around the glory of myself and then break me down with fear. I tried to block them from my friend's list, but all I got was a pop-up on my spirit screen, stating, "Unable to perform task, please try again later after surrendering to God."

So I unplugged, took a deep breath, rebooted, prayed for healing and forgiveness, then sent them both a group text that I would be on vacation for two weeks with my other friends, Humility and Faith.

I added some emojis of a peace sign and a red heart, packed a suitcase, and took off down the road.

Sometimes we all need a vacation from the everyday drama of living for ourselves, the natural agenda. Maybe a place that would remind us of a little piece of heaven...a beach, a mountain, or even just a walk down a long peaceful road. A place of wisdom and understanding, to remind us that the glory is not ours...it never was.

When I get back from vacation, I'm going to stop hanging out with Pride and Doubt; it's time to surrender to God and learn a little bit about love from Humility and Faith, my true friends. They told me I could eliminate those random pop-ups by downloading an anti-virus software called *Grace*, which is totally cool.

"If you could sit still for just a moment, I want to take a photo of your heart. This camera has lenses with spiritual vision, and it will show me the Man you are going to become when you grow up.

"My dad says the heart tells a story about trust and honesty, about respect and the true character of a person, and as a girl, he says I should always look for that.

"I'm going to zoom in on the part that Mom says is the key to a loving relationship, the unselfish, humbling, and giving part. It's near the center of the heart that God blesses when we pray to him.

"I hope it turns out to be a pretty picture because I want to put it in a frame next to my heart, and as we grow up together, we can look at it anytime, just to remind us that two hearts together always lead to love forever and ever."

"Okay, cool... Do you still want me to smile?"

I got an idea. Let's walk away forever.
Just to the edge of the path where the sky meets the heavens.
I got this stick; it will protect you from anything that tries to steal
away the beauty of your soul.
I got this feeling; we're going to discover a higher love
because when I hold your hand, I can feel my heart.

In the silence of your search,
you are my child of hope,
and I will guide you onward
and walk beside you.

In the secret of your pain,
you are my child of love,
and I will hold you near my heart
and cry along with you.

In the spirit of your soul,
you are my child of peace,
and I will lift you up
to see the light that shines within you.

In this world and in the next,
you will always be my child,
and I will always be with you, always.

Maybe hearts don't really break, but rather they're transformed into many different colors.
Maybe we should look at love with a new perspective,
a new interpretation from the artist's view, God's view.
Maybe there's a purpose to the pain that the portrait just isn't finished yet.
Maybe with a brush of hope and a stroke of faith, we might discover that there are many more colors
in heaven than there are colors in this world.
Maybe, just maybe, there is a beautiful masterpiece within every person's heart,
full of all the amazingly beautiful colors of love, God's love.
And maybe we just need to be still and let the artist color our hearts His way.

ABOUT THE AUTHOR

Christopher Beaudry has been a Facebook blogger for over ten years and writing poetry for over forty years. He is a father of three inspiring children and a grandfather of four. Living in the outskirts of Grand Rapids, Michigan, his approach to writing is simply relying on the gift God has handed him with a unique, creative, and heart-warming style. Christopher enjoys his spiritual calling as a greeter at City Church, Rockford, Michigan. He encourages everyone to believe in their purpose and dreams "any way the wind blows."

CPSIA information can be obtained
at www.ICGtesting.com
Printed in the USA
BVHW020648290522
637891BV00008B/9

9 781685 702069